Crown of Glory

Compiled For Meditation

CATHOLIC TREASURES
PO BOX 5034
MONROVIA, CA 91017-1734
(626) 359-4893

**Published with the Approval of the Most Reverend
Joseph P. Delaney, Bishop of Fort Worth**

I am writing to let you know that I am very pleased to give my approval to your manuscript, and hope you will have great success with this new edition. Be assured of our prayers!

+ *Joseph P. Delaney*
Bishop of Fort Worth

Sixth Edition, 2002
Published by Catholic Treasures
Monrovia, CA.

Scriptural texts have been excerpted with the approbation of the Confraternity of Christian Doctrine of the United States Catholic Conference in Washington, D.C. from the Revised Text of the Challoner-Rheims Version of the New Testament and from the Douay-Challoner edition of the Old Testament in the Confraternity Text published by the Catholic Press of Chicago (1950), as well as from the Douay translation of the Brepols Catholic Press of Turnhout, Belgium published by the Wildermann Co. of New York, Publishers to the Holy See (1935) and from The Living Bible, Catholic Edition, Coverdale House Publishers, Ltd., London (1973). Biblical texts are reproduced as verbatim composites of the verses indicated, but generally presented without the customary ellipses which signify omission of unnecessary words, in order to facilitate a more fluent reading for meditation. The New Testament narrative has been set in bold-face type to distinguish it from prophecies and applications of texts found elsewhere in the Holy Scriptures.

CONTENTS

INTRODUCTION

From **The Holy Eucharist** *and* **The Passion and Death of Jesus Christ** *by St. Alphonsus Maria Liguori:*

Before the coming of Jesus Christ, men fled away from God and, being attached to the earth, refused to unite themselves to their Creator. But the loving God has drawn them to Himself by the bonds of love, as He promised by the prophet Osee: "I will draw them with the cords of Adam, with the bonds of love" (11:4). These bonds are the benefits, the lights, the calls to His love, the promises of Paradise which He makes to us, but above all, the gift which He has bestowed upon us of Jesus Christ in the Sacrifice of the Cross and in the Sacrament of the Altar, and, finally, in the gift of His Holy Spirit.

The Holy Ghost was the great Promise made by Jesus Christ to those who love Him, when He said: "If you love Me, I will pray My Father, and He will send you the Holy Spirit, that He may always dwell in you" (John 14:15-16). For the Holy Spirit never forsakes a soul, if He is not driven away. God, then, dwells in a soul that loves Him; but He declares that He is not satisfied if we do not love Him with our whole heart. St. Augustine tells us that the Roman Senate would not admit Jesus Christ into the number of their gods, because they complained that He was a "proud god," Who would have none other beloved but Himself. And so it is. He will have no rivals in the heart that loves Him; and when He sees that He is not the only object loved, He is jealous, so-to-speak, according to what St. James writes: "What do you think the Scripture means when it says that the Holy Spirit, Whom God has placed within us, watches over us with tender jealousy?" (4:5). In short, as St. Jerome says, "Jesus is jealous!"

Before Our Redeemer breathed His last, He bowed His head, as a sign that He accepted death with full submission from the hands of His Father, and thus accomplished His humble obedience: "He humbled Himself, and was made obedient to death, even to the death of the cross" (Philip.

4

2:8). Jesus upon the cross, with His hands and feet nailed, could move no part of His body except His head; wherefore, it was necessary that He Himself, by bowing His head (which alone He could then move), should beckon to Death to come and slay Him. Jesus did not die of necessity, nor through the violence of the executioners, but because He voluntarily chose to die: to save man from the eternal death to which he had been condemned. This was already foretold by the prophet Osee: "I will deliver them from the hand of death; from death I will redeem them. O death, I will be thy death!" (13:14). How, then, was Jesus Christ the death of death? Because, by His death, Our Savior conquered death and destroyed the death which had resulted from sin. Therefore, the Apostle writes: "Death is swallowed up in victory!" (I Cor. 15:54). This was the victory of Jesus, since by dying He banished sin from the world and consequently delivered it from eternal death, to which the whole human race was subjected. This was the victory of the cross, on which Jesus, the Author of Life, dying, by His death acquired life for us. Whence, the Church sings of the cross that by it "Life endured death, and by death brought forth life!"

Thus, the Divine Priest, Who was both priest and victim, sacrificing His life for the salvation of the men He loved, completed the great sacrifice of the cross and accomplished the work of human redemption. Thus, death, which was an object of pain and dread, was changed by the death of Jesus into a passage from a state of peril, of eternal misery, into one of security, of eternal blessedness, and from the miseries of this life to the boundless delights of Paradise!

Let us then take heed, O Christian souls, while we are in this exile, not to look at death as a misfortune, but as the end of our pilgrimmage, which is full of difficulties and dangers, and as the beginning of our eternal happiness, which we hope one day to attain through the merits of Jesus Christ.

Amen.

IN THE HEART OF THE EARTH

A sign shall not be given this
wicked generation but the sign of
Jonas the prophet. For as Jonas was
in the belly of the whale three days and
three nights, so shall the Son of Man be
in the heart of the earth three days and
three nights. *Matthew 12:39-40*

And the next day the chief priests and the Pharisees went together to Pilate, saying: "Sir, we have remembered that that seducer said, while He was still alive: After three days, I will rise again. Command, therefore, the sepulchre to be guarded until the third day; lest perhaps His disciples come and steal Him away, and say to the people: He is risen from the dead, and the last imposture will be worse than the first ..."

Pilate said to them: "You have a guard; go, guard it as well as you know how ..."

And departing, they made the sepulchre secure, sealing the stone, and setting guards.

Matthew 27:62-66

THE RESURRECTION

Christ died for our sins according to the Scriptures ... and He rose again the third day according to the Scriptures.

I Cor. 15:3-4

For He shall be delivered to the Gentiles, and shall be mocked and scourged and spit upon; and after they have scourged Him, they will put Him to death; and the third day He shall rise again.   *Luke 18:33*

On that day, the Root of Jesse shall rise up, and His sepulchre shall be glorious.   *Romans 15:12; Isaias 11:10*

Christ is risen from the dead, the firstfruits of those who sleep; for by a man came death, and by a Man came the resurrection from the dead. And as in Adam all die, so also in Christ shall all be made to live.
I Corinthians 15:20-23

Christ died once for our sins, the Just for the unjust, that He might offer us to God, being put to death in the flesh indeed, but enlivened in the spirit.   *I Peter 3:18*

Then shall thy Light break forth as the morning, and thy Health shall speedily arise; thy Justice shall go before thy face, and the glory of the Lord shall gather thee up. Then shall the Lord declare: "Here I am!"

Isaias 58:8-9

The Lord Jesus Christ is risen again from the dead! *II Timothy 2:8*

If Christ be not risen again, then our preaching is in vain, and your faith is also vain. *I Corinthians 15:14*

I lay down My life that I may take it up again. No man taketh it away from Me, but I lay it down of Myself; and I have the power to lay it down and the power to take it up again. This commandment have I received from My Father.

John 10:17-18

For, after three days, I will rise again!
Matthew 27: 63

And the graves were opened, and many bodies of the saints who had been sleeping arose; and, coming out of the tombs after His resurrection, they came into the Holy City and appeared to many.

Matthew 27:52-53

Arise, O my Glory! ...

I will, I will arise early.   *Psalm 56:8-9*

Behold My Mother!   *Matthew 12:49*

Now, when Jesus had risen from the dead, early on the first day of the week as it began to dawn, behold: there was a great earthquake. For an angel of the Lord descended from Heaven and, coming, rolled back the stone. And the angel's countenance was like lightning, and his raiment as snow. *Mark 16:9; Matthew 28:1-3*

Thou has caused judgment to be heard from Heaven when God arose: the earth trembled, and was still. *Psalm 75:9-10*

And for fear of the angel, the guards were struck with terror, and became like dead men. *Matthew 28:4*

Let God arise, let His enemies be scattered; let those who hate Him flee from before His face. *Psalm 67:2*

Now, behold, some of the guards came into the City and told the chief priests all that had happened. And they, being assembled together with the elders and having taken counsel, gave a great sum of money to the soldiers, telling them: "Say: His disciples came by night and stole Him away while we were asleep. And if the Governor shall hear of this, we will persuade him, and keep you out of trouble." So the guards took the money and did as they were instructed: and this story has been spread abroad among the Jews even unto the present day.

Matthew 28:11-15

For all things obey money. *Ecclesiastes 10:19*

WOMEN AT THE TOMB

And when the Sabbath was past, Mary Magdalen, and Mary the mother of James, and Salome bought sweet spices so that they might go and anoint Jesus. And very early in the morning, on the first day of the week, they came to the tomb, taking the spices they had prepared, when the sun had just risen. *Mark 16:1-2; Luke 24:1*

For, unto you who fear My name the Sun of Justice shall arise.

Malachias 4:2

And they were saying one to another: "Who will roll back the stone from the entrance of the tomb for us?" And looking up, they saw that the stone had been rolled back, for it was very large. *Mark 16:3-4*

And entering into the sepulchre, they saw a young man sitting on the right side, clothed in a white robe, and they were astonished. And the angel said to the women: "Do not be afraid, for I know that you seek Jesus, Who was crucified. He is not here, for He is risen as He said."

Mark 16:5; Matthew 28:5-6

And the angel said to them: "Peace be to you! Fear not!"   *Tobias 13:17*

Come, see the place where the Lord was laid. *St. Matthew 28:6*

But go quickly, and tell His disciples and Peter that He has risen; and behold: He goes before you into Galilee, and there you shall see Him, as He told you. *Mark 16:7; Matthew 28:7*

And it came to pass, while the women were wondering what to make of this, behold: two men stood by them in shining apparel. And, as they were struck with fear and bowed their faces to the ground, they said unto them: "Why do you seek the living among the dead? He is not here, but is risen. Remember how He spoke to you while He was still in Galilee, saying that the Son of Man must be betrayed into the hands of sinful men, and be crucified, and on the third day rise again."

Mark 16:5; Matthew 28:5-6; Luke 24:4-7

For Jesus began to show His disciples that He must go to Jerusalem and suffer many things from the ancients and scribes and chief priests, and be put to death, and the third day rise again. *Mark 16:21*

"Lay up in your heart these words," He told them; "for it shall come to pass that the Son of Man shall be delivered into the hands of men."

Luke 9:44

And when they were together in Galilee, Jesus said to His disciples: "The Son of Man shall be betrayed into the hands of men; and they shall kill Him, and the third day He shall rise again." *Matthew 17:21-22*

Therefore, departing quickly from the tomb in fear and great joy, the women ran to tell His disciples. *Matthew 28:8*

THE LORD HAS RISEN!

Mary Magdalen ran and came to Simon Peter and to the other disciple whom Jesus loved, and said to them: "They have taken away the Lord out of the sepulchre, and we do not know where they have laid Him!"

John 20:2

So Peter arose and went out with the other disciple, and they both ran together to the tomb. *John 20:3-4; Luke 24:12*

And that other disciple outran Peter and arrived at the sepulchre first. And, when he had stooped down, he saw the linen cloths lying there; nevertheless, he did not go in.

Then Simon Peter came, following him; and, stooping down, he beheld the linen cloths laid there, and the napkins that had been around His head lying not with the linen cloths, but separate, folded up in a place by itself. Then that other disciple who had arrived first at the sepulchre, also went in, and he saw and believed.

John 20:6-8; Luke 24:12

But Peter went away from the sepulchre wondering within himself at that which had come to pass. For as yet they did not understand the Scripture, that He must rise again from the dead.

Luke 24:12; John 20:9

They did not understand this word, and it was hidden from them so that they did not perceive it. And they were afraid to ask Him about it.

Luke 9:45

The disciples, therefore, departed again to their home. But Mary remained at the sepulchre outside, weeping. *John 20:10-11*

CHRIST APPEARS TO MARY MAGDALEN

Now, while she was weeping, Mary stooped down and looked into the tomb; and she saw two angels in white sitting, one at the head and one at the foot, where the body of Jesus had been laid.

They said to her: "Woman, why are you weeping?" She said to them: "Because they have taken away my Lord, and I know not where they have laid Him." *John 20:11-13*

I sought Him Whom my soul loveth; I sought Him and did not find Him. Therefore do I weep, and my eyes run down with water. Have you seen Him Whom my soul loveth? *Canticles 3:1,3; Lamentations 1:16*

And when she had said this, she turned around and beheld Jesus standing there, but she did not know that it was Jesus.

Jesus said to her: "Woman, why are you weeping? Whom do you seek?"
John 20:14-15

Thinking He was the gardener, Mary said to Him: "Sir, if you have taken Him from here, tell me where you have laid Him, and I will take Him away."
John 20:15

Jesus said to her: "Mary!"

Turning, she said to Him: "Rabboni!"
John 20:16

Jesus said to her: "Do not touch Me, for I have not yet ascended to My Father. But go to My brethren, and say to them: I ascend to My Father and to your Father, to My God and your God."
John 20:17

For both He Who sanctifies and they who are sanctified are all one. For which reason, He is not ashamed to call them brethren.   *Hebrews 2:11*

And behold, Jesus met the women, saying: "All hail!" And they approached, and took hold of His feet and adored Him. Then Jesus said to them: "Fear not. Go, take word to My brethren that they are to set out for Galilee; there they shall see Me." *Matthew 28:9-10*

And having got back from the sepulchre, they told all these things to the Eleven and to all the rest. And it was Mary Magdalen, and Joanna, and Mary of James, and the other women who were with them who told these things to the Apostles. But this tale seemed to them to be nonsense, and they did not believe the women. *Luke 24:9-11*

But Mary Magdalen declared unto the disciples: "I have seen the Lord, and these things He said to me!" *John 20:18*

Yet they, hearing that He was alive, and had been seen by her, did not believe it. *Mark 16:11*

O you of little faith! Why did you doubt? *Matthew 14:31*

THE ROAD TO EMMAUS

And behold, two of the disciples were going that very day to a town sixty stadia from Jerusalem named Emmaus; and they were talking together of all these things that had happened. And it came to pass that, while they were conversing and arguing together, Jesus Himself also drew near and went along with them; but their eyes were held so that they would not recognize Him. And He said to them: "What are these discourses you are holding with one another as you walk, and are sad?" And one of them named Cleophas answered and said to Him: "Are you only a stranger in Jerusalem and do not know the things that have been done there in these days?" And Jesus replied: "What things?" And they said to Him: "Concerning Jesus of Nazareth, Who was a prophet, mighty in work and word before God and all the people; and how our chief priests and princes delivered Him up to be condemned to death, and crucified Him. But we were hoping it was He Who would have redeemed Israel. And now, besides all this, today is the third day since these things came to pass. Yes, and certain women of our company, who were at the sepulchre before it was light, also astounded us and, not finding His body, came saying that they had also seen a vision of angels who say that He is alive. So, some of our people went to the tomb and found it just as the women had said, but Him they did not find."

Luke 24:13-24

Then Jesus said to them: "O foolish and slow of heart to believe in all things which the prophets have spoken! Ought not Christ to have suffered these things, and thus enter into His glory?" And beginning then with Moses and all the prophets, He expounded to them the things referring to Himself in all the Scriptures. *Luke 24:25-27*

For all the prophets who have spoken, from Samuel and afterwards, have spoken of these days. *Acts 3:24*

And they drew near to the village where they were going, and He made as though He would go farther. But they constrained Him, saying: "Stay with us, for it is getting on towards evening, and the day is now far spent." And He went in with them.

Luke 24:28-29

Behold, I stand at the door and knock. If any man will hear My voice, and open the door to Me, I will come in and sup with him.

Apocalypse 3:20

And it came to pass, whilst He was at table with them, that He took bread, and blessed, and broke, and gave it to them …

... And their eyes were opened, and they recognized Him; and He vanished out of their sight.

Luke 24:30-31

AN ETERNAL SUPPER

And the two disciples said to one another: "Was not our heart burning within us while He was speaking on the road and explaining to us the Scriptures?" And, rising up that very hour, they returned to Jerusalem, and they found the Eleven and those who were with them gathered together declaring: "The Lord has risen indeed, and has appeared to Simon!" And they themselves began to relate what had happened on the way, and how they had recognized Him in the breaking of the bread ... and they remembered His words ...

Luke 24:32-35; 8

... Jesus took bread, gave thanks, and blessed and broke; and gave to His disciples, saying: "Take ye and eat. This is My body, which is given for you. Do this for a commemoration of Me." And taking the chalice, He gave thanks and gave to them, saying: "Drink ye all of this; for this is My blood of the new testament which shall be shed for many unto remission of sins ..."

Matthew 26:26-28; Luke 22:19

I am the living bread which came down from Heaven. If any man eat of this bread, he shall live forever; and the bread that I will give is My flesh, for the life of the world. Amen, amen, I say unto you: unless you eat the flesh of the Son of Man and drink His blood, you shall not have life in you. He who eats My flesh and drinks My blood has everlasting life: and I will raise him up on the last day. For My flesh is meat indeed, and My blood is drink indeed.

John 6:51-52,53-56

The chalice of benediction which we bless, is it not the Communion of the blood of Christ? And the bread which we break, is it not the partaking of the body of the Lord?

I Corinthians 10:16

For, from the rising of the sun even unto its going down, My name will be great among the Gentiles, and all around the world there shall be sacrifice, and there shall be offered to My name a clean oblation.

Malachias 1:11

Therefore, whosoever shall eat this bread or drink the chalice of the Lord unworthily shall be guilty of the body and blood of the Lord ... for, he who eats and drinks unworthily eats and drinks damnation unto himself, not discerning the body of the Lord.

I Corinthians 11:27,29

THROUGH CLOSED DOORS

Now, when it was late that same day, the first day of the week, and the doors where the disciples were gathered together had been shut for fear of the Jews, Jesus came and stood in the midst of them, and said: "Peace be to you! It is I; do not be afraid!"

John 20:19; Luke 24:36

But they were startled and panic-stricken and thought that they were seeing a ghost. *Luke 24:37*

And Jesus upbraided them for their lack of faith and their hardness of heart, because they had not believed those who had seen Him after He had risen. *Mark 16:14*

45

And He said to them: "Why are you troubled? And why do doubts arise in your hearts? See My hands and feet, that it is I Myself. Handle Me and see; for a spirit does not have flesh and bones, as you see Me to have." And when He had said this, He showed them His hands and His feet. *Luke 24:38-40*

Christ, Who was from the beginning, we have heard, we have seen with our eyes, we have looked upon, and our hands have handled: the Word of Life! *I John 1:1*

However, since they still did not believe and marvelled for joy, Jesus said: "Have you anything here to eat?" And they offered Him a piece of broiled fish, and a honeycomb. And, when He had eaten in their presence, He took what remained and gave it to them. *Luke 24:41-43*

**The disciples therefore rejoiced at
the sight of the Lord.** *John 20:20*

And He said to them: "These are the words which I spoke to you while I was still with you, that all things written in the Law of Moses and in the prophets and in the Psalms concerning Me must necessarily be fulfilled." Then He opened their understanding so that they might understand the Scriptures. And He said to them: "Thus is it written, and thus did it behoove Christ to suffer and on the third day to rise again from the dead; that penance and the remission of sins should be preached in His name to all nations, beginning at Jerusalem."

Luke 24:44-48

Jesus therefore said to them again: "Peace be to you. As the Father has sent Me, I also send you." When He had said this, He breathed upon them, and said: "Receive the Holy Ghost. Whose sins you shall forgive, they are forgiven them. And whose sins you shall retain, they are retained."

John 20:21-23

DOUBTING THOMAS

Now, Thomas, one of the Twelve who is called The Twin, was not with them when Jesus came. The other disciples therefore said to him: "We have seen the Lord!" But he said to them: "Unless I see in His hands the print of the nails, and put my finger into the place of the nails, and put my hand into His side, I will not believe." *John 20:24-25*

And after eight days, the disciples of Jesus were again inside, and Thomas was with them. Jesus came, the doors being locked, and stood in their midst and said: "Peace be to you!" Then He said to Thomas: "Put your finger in here, and see My hands; and bring here your hand and put it into My side. And be not faithless, but believing!"

John 20:26-27

Have the faith of God! *Mark 11:22*

Thomas answered and said to Him: "My Lord and my God!"
John 20:28

Because thou hast seen Me, Thomas, thou hast believed. Blessed are they who have not seen, and have believed.
John 20:29

VISION AT THE LAKE

After this, Jesus manifested Himself to His disciples again at the Sea of Tiberius in this manner: There were together Simon Peter and Thomas, called the Twin, and Nathanael, and the sons of Zebedee, and two others of His disciples. Simon Peter said to them: "I am going fishing." They replied: "We are also coming with you." And they went forth and got into the boat; and that night they caught nothing. *John 21:1-3*

But when day was now breaking, Jesus stood on the shore; nevertheless, the disciples did not know that it was Jesus. Jesus then said to them: "Children! Have you any fish?" They answered Him: "No!" He said to them: "Cast the net on the right side of the boat, and you will find them."

They cast, therefore, and were now unable to draw up the net because of the great number of fish. The disciple whom Jesus loved therefore said to Peter: "It is the Lord!" Simon Peter, hearing that it was the Lord, girt his tunic around him, for he was naked, and cast himself into the sea. But the other disciples came with the boat, for they were not far from land, dragging the net full of fishes. *John 21:4-8*

As soon as they came to land, they saw hot coals prepared, and a fish laid thereon, and bread. Jesus said to them: "Bring here some of the fish you have just now caught." Simon Peter went aboard and hauled the net to shore, full of large fish: one-hundred-and-fifty-three in number. And, although there were so many, the net was not broken.

... Jesus said to them: "Come and eat." And none of those who were eating dared to ask Him: "Who are you?" knowing that it was the Lord.   *John 21:9-12*

I am the Good Shepherd. I know Mine, and Mine know Me. *John 10:14*

But if any man know not, he shall not be known.   *I Corinthians 14:28*

KEYS TO THE KINGDOM

Then Jesus said to Simon Peter: "Simon, son of John, do you love Me more than these others?" He said to Him: "Yea, Lord, You know that I love You." He said to him: "Feed My lambs." He said to him again: "Simon, son of John, do you love Me?" He said to Him: "Yea, Lord! You know that I love You!" He said to him: "Feed My lambs." He said to him a third time: "Simon, son of John, do you love Me?" Peter was grieved that Jesus had asked him a third time "Do you love Me?" And he said to Him: "Lord, You know all things; You know that I love You!" He said to him: "Feed My sheep." *John 21:15-17*

I will set up one Shepherd over My flock, and he shall feed them: he shall feed them and shall be their shepherd. *Ezechiel 34:22-23*

Jesus asked His disciples: "Who do men say the Son of Man is?" And they said: "Some say John the Baptist, some others Elias, and others Jeremias or one of the prophets." Jesus said to them: "But who do you say that I am?" Simon Peter answered and said: "Thou art Christ, the Son of the living God." And Jesus, answering, said to him: "Blessed art thou, Simon son of John, because flesh and blood hath not revealed it to thee, but My Father Who is in Heaven. And I say to thee: Thou art Peter; and upon this Rock I will build My Church, and the gates of Hell shall not prevail against it. And I will give to thee the keys to the Kingdom of Heaven. And whatsoever thou shalt bind upon earth, it shall be bound also in Heaven; and whatsoever thou shalt loose on earth, it shall be loosed also in Heaven." *Matthew 16:13-19*

I am the good shepherd. The good shepherd giveth His life for His sheep. But the hireling, whose own the sheep are not, sees the wolf coming and flies, because he has no concern for the sheep. I am the good shepherd, and I lay down My life for My sheep. And other sheep I have, that are not of this fold: them also I must bring, and they shall hear My voice, and there shall be one fold and one shepherd. *John 10:11-16*

This is now the third time that Jesus was manifested to His disciples after He had risen from the dead.
John 21:14

He had been seen by Cephas and, after that, by the Eleven. Then He was seen by more than five hundred brethren at one time. After that, He was seen by James, and then by all the Apostles.
I Corinthians 15:5-7

O Lord, Thou art among this people, and art seen by them face-to-face!
Numbers 14:14

THE GREAT COMMISSION

Then Jesus spoke to the disciples, saying: "All power in Heaven and on earth has been given to Me. Go, therefore, teach ye all nations, baptizing them in the name of the Father, and of the Son, and of the Holy Ghost.

Matthew 28:18-19

63

Go into the whole world, and preach the Gospel to every creature, teaching them to observe all things whatsoever I have commanded you.

Mark 16:15; Matthew 28:20

He who believes and is baptized shall be saved, but he who does not believe shall be condemned. *Mark 16:16*

Without the faith, it is impossible to please God. *Hebrews 11:6*

Unless one be born again of water and the Holy Ghost, he cannot enter into the kingdom of God. *John 3:5*

And behold, I am with you all days, even unto the consummation of the world.

Matthew 28:20

For Jesus continueth forever, and hath an everlasting priesthood, whereby He is also able to save forever those who come to God by Him; always living to make intercession for us. For, it was fitting that we should have such a High Priest: holy, innocent, undefiled, separated from sinners, and made higher than the Heavens ...

Having, therefore, a great High Priest Who hath passed into the Heavens, Jesus the Son of God, let us hold fast to our confession. For we do not have a High Priest Who cannot have compassion on our infirmities, but One tempted in all things as we are, without sin. Let us go, therefore, to the throne of grace with confidence, that we may obtain mercy.

Hebrews 7:24-26;4:14-16

67

And Jesus commanded His disciples that they should not depart from Jerusalem, but should wait for the Promise of the Father.   *Acts 1:4*

For I will send forth upon you the Promise of My Father. But wait here in the City until you are clothed with power from on high.   *Luke 24:49*

Now I go to Him Who sent Me ... And I tell you truly: it is expedient to you that I go; for if I do not go, the Paraclete will not come to you; but if I go, I will send Him to you.   *John 16:5-7*

For John indeed baptized with water, but you shall be baptized with the Holy Ghost not many days from now.   *Acts 1:5*

And the Paraclete, the Holy Ghost, Whom the Father will send in My name, He will teach you all things, and bring all things to your mind whatsoever I shall have said to you ... Now, I have told you this before it comes to pass; that, when it shall come to pass, you may believe.
    John 14:26,29

Thou shalt send forth Thy Spirit, and they shall be created: and Thou shalt renew the face of the earth!   *Psalm 103:30*

THE ASCENSION

They, therefore, who had assembled asked Him, saying: "Lord, will You at this time restore the kingdom to Israel again?" But He said to them: "It is not for you to know the times nor the moments which the Father has fixed by His own authority. But you shall receive the power of the Holy Ghost coming upon you, and you shall be witnesses unto Me in Jerusalem, and in all Judea and Samaria, and even unto the uttermost ends of the earth." *Acts 1:6-8*

For there are no speeches or languages where their voices are not heard. Their sound hath gone forth unto all the earth, and their words unto the ends of the world. *Psalm 18:4-5*

Yes, truly: their sound hath gone forth into all the earth, and their words unto the ends of the whole world! *Romans 10:18*

70

And, while they looked on, He was raised up.
Acts 3:26;1:9

And, lifting up His hands, He blessed them; and, while He blessed them, He departed from them, and was carried up to Heaven. *Luke 24:50-51*

You shall see the Son of Man ascending up to Heaven again! I go to My Father, and you shall see Me no longer! *John 6:63;16:10*

You shall see the Son of Man ascending up to Heaven again! I go to My Father, and you shall see Me no longer! *John 6:63;16:10*

And a cloud received Him out of their sight, while they were beholding Him going up to Heaven.
Acts 1:9-10

Lift up your gates, O ye princes, and be ye lifted up, O eternal gates! And the King of Glory shall enter in!
Psalm 23:7

O clap your hands, all ye nations: shout unto God with the voice of triumph! God ascends His throne with jubilee; and takes His seat as King amid trumpet-blasts!
Psalm 46:2,6

God set Him above all principality, and power, and virtue, and dominion, and above every name that is named, not only in this world, but also in the world which is to come. Neither is there salvation in any other; for there is no other name under Heaven given to men whereby we must be saved. *Ephesians 1:20-22; Acts 4:12*

And while the disciples were gazing at Him going up into Heaven, behold: two men stood beside them in white garments, and said to them: "Ye men of Galilee, why do you stand looking up to Heaven? This Jesus, Who has been taken up from you into Heaven, shall come as you have seen Him going." *Acts 1:10*

For, as the lightning that lightens from under heaven shines unto the parts that are under heaven, so shall the Son of Man be in His day.
Luke 17:24

And then shall appear the sign of the Son of Man in Heaven: and then shall the tribes of the earth mourn; and they shall see the Son of Man coming in the clouds of heaven with much power and majesty. And He shall send His angels with a trumpet and a great voice: and they shall gather together His elect from the four winds and from the farthest parts of the heavens to the utmost bounds of them. *Matthew 24:30-31*

And the disciples, adoring, went back into Jerusalem with great joy from the Mount called Olivet, which is near Jerusalem. *Acts 1:12*

DESCENT OF THE HOLY GHOST

And when they had returned to Jerusalem, they went up into an upper
room where were staying Peter and John, James and Andrew, Philip
and Thomas, Bartholomew and Matthew, James of Alpheus, Simon the
Zealot, and Jude, the brother of James. All these were persevering with
one mind in prayer with the women, and with Mary the Mother of
Jesus. *Acts 1:13-14*

Know ye that the Lord will hear your prayers if you continue
with perseverance in fastings and prayers in the sight of the
Lord. *Judith 4:11*

Peter rose up in the midst of the brethren in those days, and said: "Men, brethren! The Scriptures, which the Holy Ghost has declared before by the mouth of David, must necessarily be fulfilled concerning Judas who was the leader of those who arrested Jesus. He had been numbered among us, and had obtained a portion of this ministry. And he possessed indeed a field with the reward of his iniquity and, being hanged, burst asunder in the middle, and all his bowels gushed out. And it became known to all the inhabitants of Jerusalem, so that this field came to be called Haceldama in their language, that is: the Field of Blood. For it is written in the Book of Psalms: Let their habitation become desolate; and let there be no one to dwell in it; and his bishopric let another man take." *Acts 1:15-20*

May he go out condemned; and may his prayer be turned to sin. May his days be few, and his bishopric let another man take. *Psalm 108:7-8*

"Wherefore: one of these men who has been in our company all the time the Lord Jesus came in and went out among us must be made a witness along with us of His resurrection." And they appointed two men: Joseph, called Barsabbas, who was surnamed The Just, and Matthias. And they drew lots between them, and the lot fell upon Matthias, and he was counted among the eleven Apostles. *Acts 1:21-26*

And when the days of
Pentecost were draw-
ing to a close, the dis-
ciples were all togeth-
er in one place. And
suddenly, there came
a sound from Heav-
en, as of a mighty
wind blowing; and it
filled the whole
house where they
were sitting. And
there appeared to
them parted tongues
as of fire, which set-
tled upon every one
of them. And they
were all filled with
the Holy Ghost.

Acts 2:1-4

And when the Spirit
had rested upon
them, they prophes-
ied; nor did they cease
ever afterwards. Oh,
that all the people
might prophesy, and
that the Lord would
give them all His
Spirit!

Numbers 11:25,29

Now, there were staying in Jerusalem Jews, devout men, from every nation under heaven. And the multitude came together and were bewildered in mind, because every man heard them speaking in his own language. They were all amazed, and marvelled, saying: "Behold, are not all these who speak Galileans? And how have we each heard his own language in which he was born? For we have heard them speak in our own languages of the wonderful works of God!" And they were all amazed and wondered, saying one to another: "What does this mean?"

Acts 2:5-12

But Peter, standing up with the Eleven, lifted up his voice and cried out to them: "Ye men of Juda! And all you who dwell in Jerusalem! Give ear to my words! For this is what was spoken through the prophet Joel!

Acts 2:14-18

And it shall come to pass that I will pour out My Spirit upon all flesh; and your sons and daughters shall prophesy: your old men shall dream dreams and your young men shall see visions. Moreover, upon My servants and handmaids will I pour forth My Spirit in those days.

Joel 2:28-29

PETER PREACHES TO THE MULTITUDES

You men of Israel, hear these words! Jesus of Nazareth, a man approved by God among you by miracles and wonders and signs, which God worked through Him in the midst of you all, this same Jesus you have crucified and slain by the hands of wicked men. But God has raised Him up, having loosed the sorrows of Hell. For David says, concerning Him: "I saw the Lord before my face always, because He is at my right hand, that I may not be moved. This is why my heart has made merry and my tongue has rejoiced; moreover, my flesh shall also rest in hope, because Thou wilt not abandon My soul to Hell, nor permit Thy Holy One to undergo corruption."

Brethren, the patriarch David both died and was buried, and his tomb is with us to this present day. Therefore, since he was a prophet, David spoke of the resurrection of Christ; for neither was He left in Hell, nor did His flesh see corruption. This Jesus, God hath raised up, of which we are all witnesses. Therefore, being exalted by the right hand of God, and having received the Promise of the Holy Ghost, He hath poured forth this Spirit which you see and hear. For David did not ascend into Heaven; yet he himself says: "The Lord said to my Lord: Sit Thou on My right hand until I make Thy enemies Thy footstool." Therefore, God hath made both Lord and Christ this same Jesus, Whom you have crucified."

Acts 2:22-36

Now, when the people heard these things, they were pierced to the heart, and said to Peter and to the rest of the Apostles: "What shall we do, men and brethren?" But Peter said to them: "Do penance and be baptized, every one of you, in the name of Jesus Christ, for the remission of your sins; and you will receive the gift of the Holy Ghost...

For the Promise is to you and to your children, and to all who are far off, whomsoever the Lord our God shall call to Himself." *Acts 2:37-39*

They who are children of the Promise are the children of God, not those who are children of the flesh. However, you are not in the flesh, but rather in the Spirit, if it be that the Spirit of God dwells in you. Now, if any man does not have the Spirit of Christ, he is none of His.

Romans 9:8;8:9

And with very many other words Peter bore witness and exhorted them, saying: "Save yourselves from this perverse generation!" *Acts 2:40*

They who received his word, therefore, were baptized; and there were added that day about three thousand souls. And the Lord added daily to the Church those being saved.

Acts 2:41,47

And they continued steadfastly in the teaching of the Apostles, and in the Communion of the breaking of the bread, and in prayers. And fear came upon every soul; many wonders also and signs were done by the Apostles in Jerusalem, and great fear came upon all men. And continuing daily with one accord in the Temple, they met in groups in their homes for Communion, and shared their food with gladness and simplicity of heart, praising God, and having favor with all the people. *Acts 2:42-47*

And when they had prayed, the building trembled wherein they were gathered; and they were all filled with the Holy Ghost and spoke the word of God with boldness. And the multitude of believers had but one heart and soul. And with great power the Apostles gave testimony of the resurrection of Our Lord Jesus Christ, and great grace was in them all. *Acts 4:31-33*

Christ is God, blessed forever! Amen. *Romans 9:5*

For the grace of God our Savior has appeared to all men who are looking for the blessed hope and coming of the glory of our great God and Savior, Jesus Christ. *Titus 2:11,13*

And going forth, they preached everywhere: the Lord working withal, and confirming the word with signs that followed. *Mark 16:20*

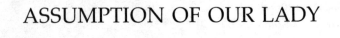

ASSUMPTION OF OUR LADY

We who live are always delivered unto death for Jesus' sake; that the life of Jesus may also be made manifest in our mortal flesh, knowing that He Who raised up Jesus will also raise us up with Jesus.

II Corinthians 4:11,14

For we are buried together with Him by Baptism into death; that, as Christ is risen from the dead by the glory of the Father, so we also may walk in newness of life.

Romans 6:4

Behold, my Beloved speaketh to me! "Arise, make haste, My love, My dove, My beautiful one, and come! For winter is now past; the rain is over and gone."

Canticles 2:10-11

Come quickly, My beloved!
Canticles 8:13

Who is she who cometh forth as the morning rising, fair as the moon, bright as the sun, terrible as an army set in battle array?

Cant. 6:9

Who is she who cometh up from the desert, flowing with delights, leaning upon her Beloved?

Cant. 8:5

O Lord, have mercy on me, and raise me up again! Thou dost revive me by reason of my innocence, and Thou hast established me in Thy sight forever!

Psalm 40:11-13

Beloved, ascend higher!   *Luke 14:10*

And the Temple of God was opened in Heaven, and the Ark of His Testament was seen in His Temple, and there came forth flashes of lightning and peals of thunder. *Apocalypse 11:19*

Arise, O Lord, into Thy resting place: Thou and the Ark which Thou has sanctified. *Psalm 131:8*

The Most High hath sanctified His own tabernacle! *Psalm 45:5*

All glorious is the King's daughter as she enters; her raiment is threaded with spun gold. *Psalm 44:14*

Kings shall stand at attention when they see thee; princes shall bow low and venerate thee for the sake of the Lord Who hath chosen thee: He, the faithful Lord, the Holy One of Israel chooses thee! *Isaias 49:7*

One is My dove, My perfect one is singular: the only one of her mother, the chosen one of her who bore her. The daughters beheld her and declared her most blessed ...

the queens and concubines saw her, and praised her. Return! Return! Return! Return, so that We may behold thee!

Canticles 6:8,12

Thou art all fair, O My love, and there is not a spot in thee. Come, My spouse, come. Thou shalt be crowned! *Canticles 4:7,8*

THE CORONATION

I was raised up like a cedar in Lebanon, like a cypress tree on Mount Sion: I was exalted like a palm tree in Cades, like a rose in Jericho.

Ecclesiasticus 24:17-18

And there was silence in Heaven, as it were for half an hour! Then I beheld, and heard the voice of many angels round about the throne.

Apocalypse 8:1;5:11

On God's right hand stands the Queen, His spouse, adorned in choicest gold, and clad in robes of many colors.   *Psalm 44:10*

Blessed art thou, O daughter, by the Lord the most high God, above all women upon earth!

Judith 13:23

For God hath so magnified thy name this day that thy praise shall not depart out of the mouth of men forever! And in every nation which shall hear thy name the God of Israel shall be magnified because of thee.

Judith 13:25,31

And a great sign appeared in Heaven: a woman clothed with the sun, and the moon was under her feet, and upon her head a crown of twelve stars.   *Apocalypse 12:1*

And the King loved her more than all other women, and she found grace and favor in His sight above all virgins; therefore, He set the royal crown upon her head and made her Queen.   *Esther 2:17*

Thou art beautiful, O My love: sweet and comely as Jerusalem, terrible as an army set in battle array. *Canticles 6:3*

Thou art the glory of Jerusalem, thou art the joy of Israel, thou art the honor of our people, and thou shalt be blessed forever! *Judith 15:10-11*

101

I am the mother of fair love, and of fear, and of knowledge, and of holy hope. In me is all grace of the way and of truth, in me is all hope of life and of virtue.   *Ecclesiasticus 24:24-25*

I am the way, and the truth, and the life. No man cometh to the Father except by Me.

John 14:6

PICTURE CREDITS

Our heartfelt acknowledgment to Msgr. William Botik, pastor of Christ the King Church, Dallas, for the awe-inspiring reproduction of Our Lord enthroned; to Our Sunday Visitor, Inc. for generous use of their masterful production, "JESUS: the Son of Man"; and to Obra Nactional de la Buena Prensa of Mexico for so many wonderful pieces found in their monumental "EL ROSARIO EN IMAGENES"; likewise, to the Rosary Album Press of Denver for their devotional "ROSARY ALBUM: A Visual and Scriptural Meditation On The Rosary"; finally, our sincerest gratitude to all those friends who generously contributed their most Glorious pictures.

We have concluded this volume, the third in our collection depicting the mysteries of Our Blessed Savior, with a drawing of the Sacred Heart of Jesus. The original hangs in the Library of Congress, Washington, D.C., having been presented by the government of France in 1899, and accepted by a formal Act of Congress that year. May the Sacred Heart give us all a share in His eternal weight of glory!

CATHOLIC TREASURES
PO BOX 5034
MONROVIA, CA 91017-1734
(626) 359-4893